Where Does Pepper Come From?

And Other Fun Facts

Where Does Pepper Come From?

By Brigitte Raab

Illustrated by Manuela Olten

Translated by
J. Alison James

Black pepper comes from
the berries of the pepper plant.
The berries are picked while still
green and then dried. Black pepper
is the most common spice in the
world, and it adds a hot, spicy taste
to food. Most pepper is grown
in India, Indonesia, Brazil,
and Malaysia.

NorthSouth
New York / London

Why do bears
hibernate in winter?

Because they can't find winter coats big enough to fit them!

In the winter there is not enough food for bears to eat. That is why they eat enough food in the fall to last them through the winter. Then they spend the coldest time of the year sleeping in caves.

Because they love to go camping!

No!

The shell of a snail protects it from predators and from the hot sun.

Because a sea captain
sprinkled salt on the water.

The salt is in the rocks and stones of the earth. Rain soaks through the ground, dissolving salt along the way. The salty water runs into streams and rivers, which carry the salt to the oceans.

Sea Salt

Sea

Because they're embarrassed about being stared at in the zoo.

No!

Flamingos eat a lot of small shrimp, crabs, and algae, which have the same red carotenoid pigment that carrots have. That's why they turn pink.

Because they love to
put it up in curlers!

Sheep's wool is naturally curly. The curls create pockets of air that keep the sheep warm in cold and windy weather.

Why isn't a whale a fish?

Because whales are too big
to fit into any aquariums.

Most fish lay eggs, but whales give birth to live babies. Whales are mammals, and whale babies drink milk from their mothers.

Why don't migrating birds get lost when they fly south in the fall?

Because they have
compasses in their beaks!

Migrating birds actually do have a kind of compass in their beaks that helps them to find their way. Birds also orient themselves by the sun and the stars.

Text and illustrations copyright © 2005 by Verlag Friedrich Oetinger, GmbH, Hamburg, Germany
English translation copyright © 2006 by North-South Books Inc., New York

First published in Germany by Verlag Friedrich Oetinger
under the title *Wo wächst der Pfeffer?*

Published in the United States, Great Britain, Canada, Australia, and New Zealand in 2006
by North-South Books Inc., an imprint of NordSüd Verlag AG, Zürich, Switzerland.
First paperback edition published in 2008 by North-South Books Inc.
Distributed in the United States by North-South Books Inc., New York.
Library of Congress Cataloging-in-Publication Data is available.
A CIP catalogue record for this book is available from The British Library.

ISBN: 978-0-7358-2070-8 (trade edition)
3 5 7 6 9 10 8 6 4 2
ISBN: 978-0-7358-2218-4 (paperback edition)
1 3 5 7 6 9 10 8 6 4 2

Printed in Belgium